CHRISTMAS PUZZLES for KIDS

Activity Book

30580PO100000051

Prophets and Prophesies

Long before Jesus was born, God had a plan to send His Son to be our Savior. God used special people called "prophets" to tell people what He planned to do. This message from God is called a "prophesy." Every word God spoke to the prophets came true.

Use your NIV Bible to match the prophets to their prophecies.
Draw the picture in the first column in the correct boxes in the second and third columns.

Prophet	Bible Verse	Prophecy
Isaiah	**Micah 5:2**	There before me was one like a son of man, coming with the clouds of heaven…. He was given authority, glory and sovereign power; all nations and people of every language worshiped him…. His kingdom is one that will never be destroyed.
David	**Zechariah 9:9**	She gave thanks to God and spoke about the child to all who were looking forward to the redemption of Jerusalem.
Daniel	**Isaiah 7:14**	But you, Bethlehem Ephrathah, though you are small among the clans of Judah, out of you will come for me one who will be ruler over Israel.
Micah	**Luke 2:38**	See, your king comes to you, righteous and victorious, lowly and riding on a donkey, on a colt, the foal of a donkey.
Zechariah	**Psalm 22:16–18**	Therefore the Lord himself will give you a sign: The virgin will conceive and give birth to a son, and will call him Immanuel.
Anna	**Daniel 7:13–14**	A pack of villains encircles me; they pierce my hands and my feet…. They divide my clothes among them and cast lots for my garment.

Answer on page 16

Names of Jesus

An angel told Joseph to give God's Son the name Jesus.
One of Isaiah's prophesies tells some of the other names that Jesus would be given.

Use the clues to solve the crossword puzzle.
Then use the words to fill in the blanks in the Bible verse at the bottom of the page.

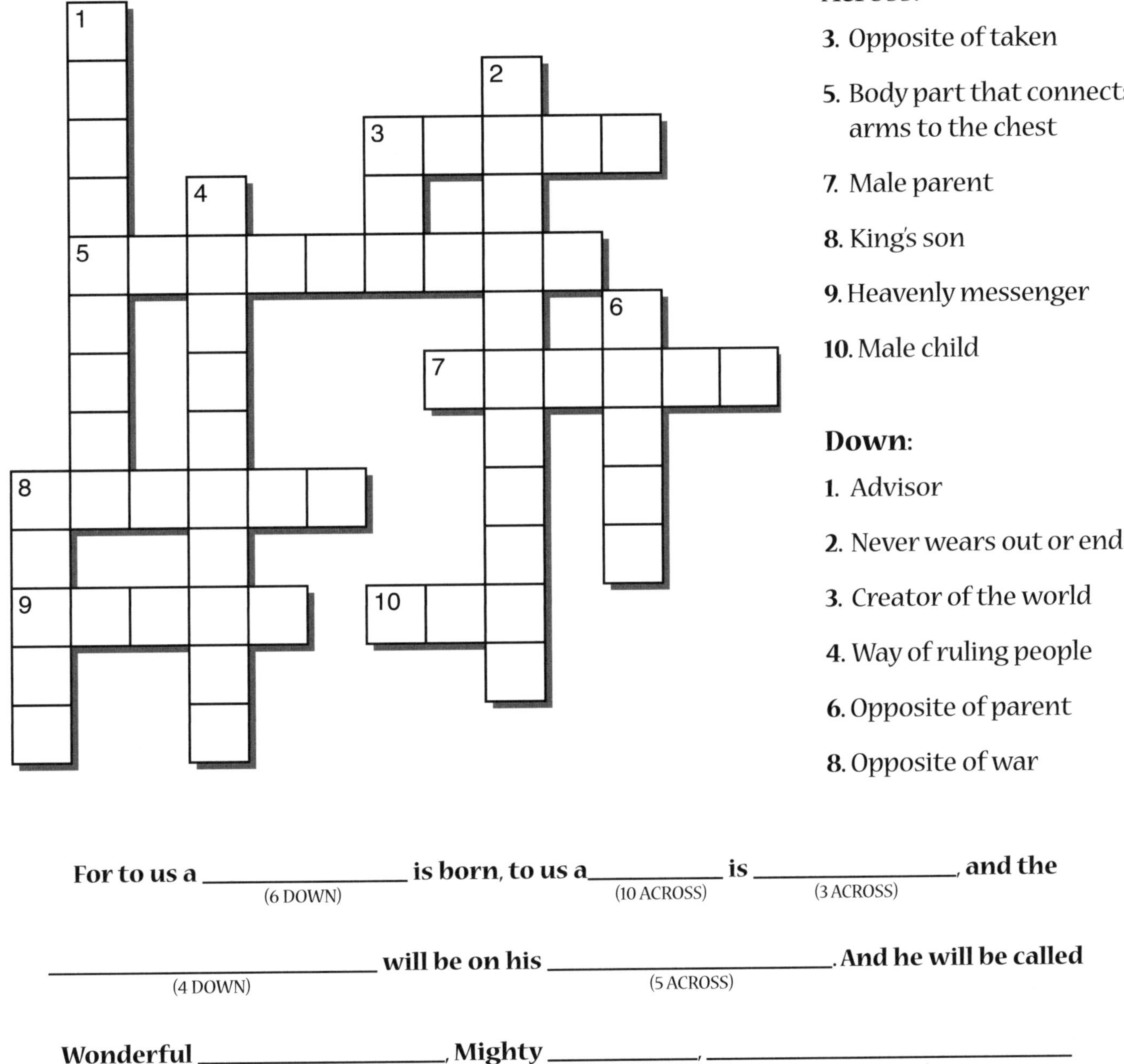

Across:

3. Opposite of taken
5. Body part that connects arms to the chest
7. Male parent
8. King's son
9. Heavenly messenger
10. Male child

Down:

1. Advisor
2. Never wears out or ends
3. Creator of the world
4. Way of ruling people
6. Opposite of parent
8. Opposite of war

For to us a __________ (6 DOWN) **is born, to us a** __________ (10 ACROSS) **is** __________ (3 ACROSS), **and the** __________ (4 DOWN) **will be on his** __________ (5 ACROSS). **And he will be called Wonderful** __________ (1 DOWN), **Mighty** __________ (3 DOWN), __________ (2 DOWN) __________ (7 ACROSS), __________ (8 ACROSS) **of** __________ (8 DOWN). ***Isaiah 9:6 (NIV)***

Answer on page 16

People in the Christmas Story

Do you remember these people from the Christmas story and what they did?

Circle the words hidden forwards, backwards, up, down, or diagonally.

K	J	E	G	X	J	D	H	Q	O	E	Z	H	T	R	F	T	S	G	S	R
F	E	K	Q	A	C	I	K	O	L	Z	N	T	G	X	M	T	D	W	S	Y
O	S	R	U	F	B	P	L	I	L	F	M	A	R	Y	K	E	R	V	G	A
X	U	Z	I	Y	P	C	Z	O	N	Y	E	R	Q	C	Q	F	E	V	O	R
P	S	O	E	W	Z	A	H	W	M	G	S	D	O	W	K	T	H	M	D	C
I	A	Z	E	C	B	C	W	I	W	D	W	P	W	U	B	V	P	V	Q	H
J	M	M	K	E	H	M	W	V	E	C	P	C	I	S	D	L	E	H	R	E
X	F	S	T	L	C	A	Q	U	R	F	W	B	U	R	W	T	H	K	A	L
C	V	H	Q	M	Z	J	R	W	S	O	P	T	M	X	I	H	S	W	Z	A
H	B	C	S	L	R	N	A	I	V	S	S	R	V	K	I	T	H	F	H	U
N	F	U	M	V	L	J	M	K	A	U	H	G	I	Z	K	G	S	T	K	S
X	C	Z	S	U	W	U	M	C	G	H	E	A	S	E	I	B	J	D	G	D
U	Q	W	G	R	O	P	M	U	D	N	Q	U	M	Y	S	L	H	O	K	G
U	I	S	A	C	I	H	A	W	S	N	I	B	C	F	L	T	O	R	F	W
C	Z	J	U	H	P	R	E	H	N	N	I	L	H	M	P	T	S	E	S	P
A	N	J	E	E	A	C	X	S	I	G	K	A	H	C	C	T	K	H	L	I
F	S	C	S	S	L	I	X	R	A	Q	F	T	G	O	A	T	A	G	K	Z
I	S	O	E	E	W	R	I	M	Y	D	Y	F	U	Z	K	A	U	N	Q	Q
Y	J	A	H	T	B	U	L	K	U	P	N	O	E	M	I	S	H	I	N	N
O	C	S	B	T	Q	C	P	G	M	Z	A	Y	Q	Z	S	N	L	K	G	A

Zechariah
Elizabeth
Mary
Joseph
Anna
Simeon
Jesus
King Herod
Shepherds
Holy Spirit
God
Caesar Augustus
Magi
Quirinius
Archelaus
Chief Priests

Answer on page 16

Christmas Story Mix-up

How well do you know the story of Jesus' birth?

Look at each picture carefully. Number them in the correct order from 1-6. Choose the correct caption from the list at the bottom of the page and write it on the lines under the picture.

Angels Praise God **Wise Men Bring Gifts** **An Angel Visits Mary**

A Trip to Bethlehem **Shepherds Visit Jesus** **Jesus Is Born!**

Answer on page 16

Christmas Angels

Around the time of Jesus' birth, many people had angelic visitors who gave them important messages from God.

Each angel has a Bible verse for you to read. On the From *line, write the name of the angel. On the* To *line, write the name of the person or persons the angel visited. On the* Message *line, write a sentence about what the angel said. When you are finished, put the angels in order from 1–6 according to where they appear in the Christmas story.*

_____ **Luke 2:13–14**

From: ____________________

To: ____________________

Message: ____________________

____

____

____

_____ **Matthew 1:20–24**

From: ____________________

To: ____________________

Message: ____________________

____

____

____

_____ **Luke 1:11–13, 19–20**

From: ____________________

To: ____________________

Message: ____________________

____

____

____

_____ **Luke 1:26–38**

From: ____________________

To: ____________________

Message: ____________________

____

____

____

_____ **Matthew 2:13**

From: ____________________

To: ____________________

Message: ____________________

____

____

____

_____ **Luke 2:8–12**

From: ____________________

To: ____________________

Message: ____________________

____

____

____

Answer on page 16

Shepherds Visit Jesus

What started out as just another night watching sheep turned out to be the most exciting night of all! The shepherds were frightened when they saw the bright light and an angel. Then they were amazed to hear the angel's good news. They hurried to Bethlehem and found Baby Jesus. Their hearts were filled with joy, and they praised God all the way home.

Help the shepherds find Jesus.

Answer on page 16

Surprise Visitors

Mary and Joseph had some unexpected visitors during the time the Christmas story took place. Do you remember them and what happened when they came?

Use the clues to solve the crossword puzzle. Hint: Look up the Bible verses if you need help.

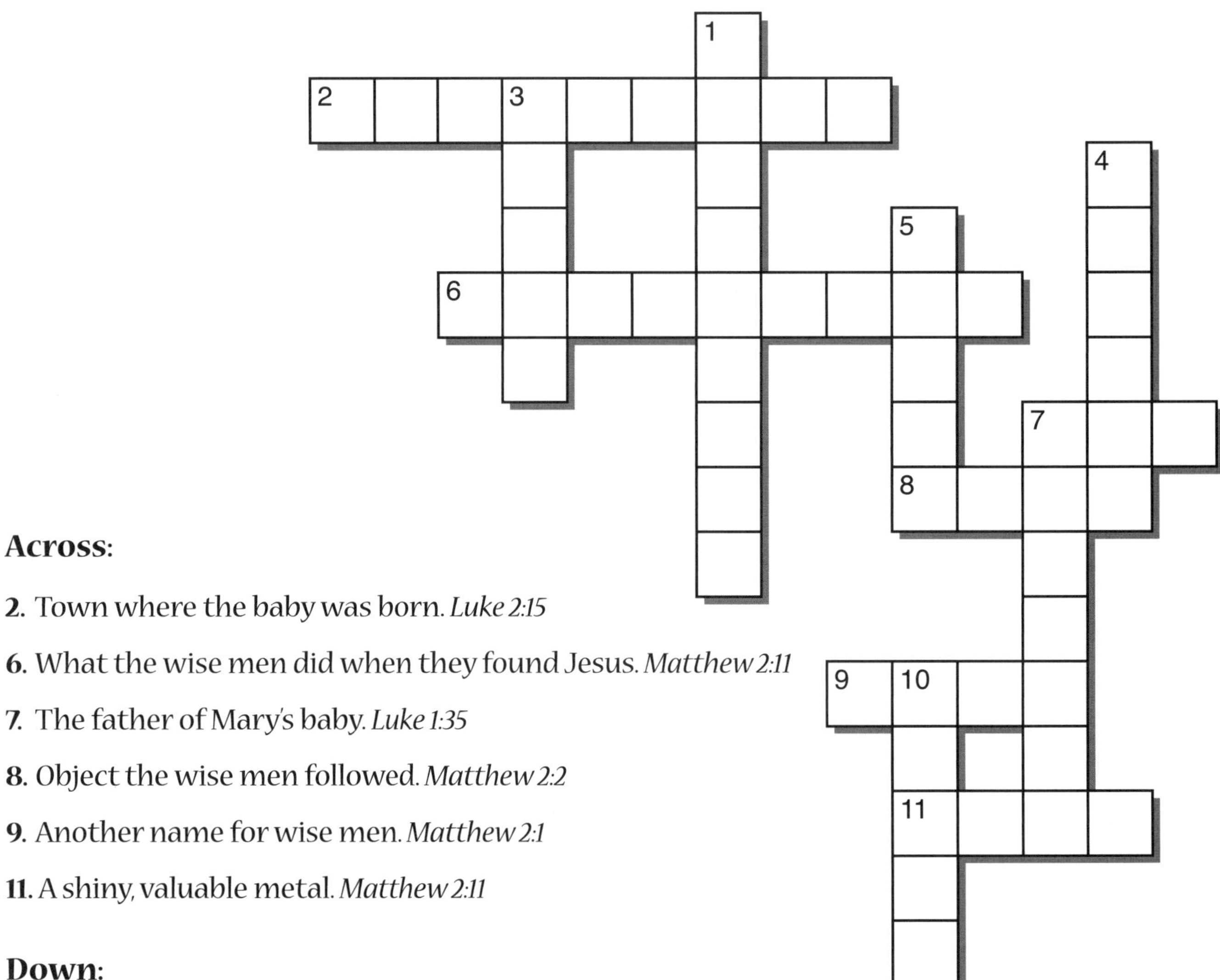

Across:

2. Town where the baby was born. *Luke 2:15*

6. What the wise men did when they found Jesus. *Matthew 2:11*

7. The father of Mary's baby. *Luke 1:35*

8. Object the wise men followed. *Matthew 2:2*

9. Another name for wise men. *Matthew 2:1*

11. A shiny, valuable metal. *Matthew 2:11*

Down:

1. Men who watch over sheep. *Luke 2:8*

3. Bad king who said he wanted to visit the child. *Matthew 2:7–8*

4. An angel said a _______ had been born. *Luke 2:11*

5. Name Joseph was told to give the baby. *Matthew 1:21*

7. Name of angel who visited Mary. *Luke 1:26–27*

10. He told Joseph that Mary would have a son. *Matthew 1:20–21*

Answer on page 16

A Message for Mary

Mary was just a young woman when the angel Gabriel told her God had chosen her to be the mother of His only Son. What did the angel say?

Use the secret code to read the Bible verses.

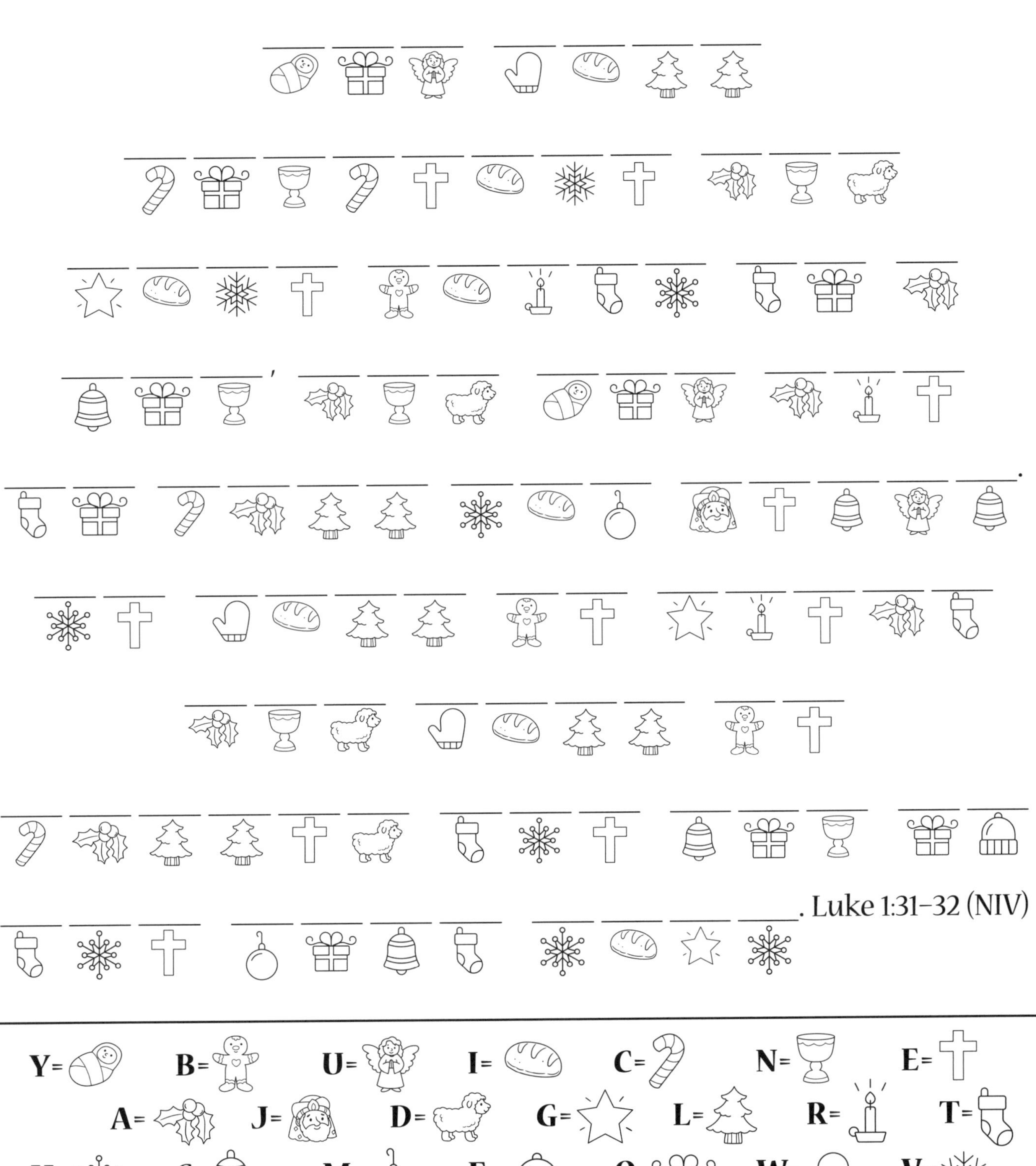

Y= B= U= I= C= N= E=

A= J= D= G= L= R= T=

H= S= M= F= O= W= V=

Answer on page 16

Who Said It?

The Bible has many beautiful verses that we enjoy reading during the Christmas season year after year. See if you can remember who said these statements from the Christmas story.

Use your NIV Bible to match the person to their famous quote. Then match the quote to the Scripture reference. Draw the picture in the first column in the correct boxes in the second and third columns.

Speaker	Quote	Bible Verse
Mary	"I bring you good news that will cause great joy for all the people."	Luke 1:42
Magi	"Blessed are you among women, and blessed is the child you will bear!"	Luke 2:10
Angel	"You will conceive and give birth to a son, and you are to call him Jesus."	Luke 1:46-47
Shepherds	"Glory to God in the highest heaven, and on earth peace to those on whom his favor rests."	Luke 1:31
Gabriel	"My soul glorifies the Lord and my spirit rejoices in God my Savior."	Luke 2:14
Elizabeth	"You may now dismiss your servant in peace. For my eyes have seen your salvation."	Matthew 2:2
Heavenly Host	"Let's go to Bethlehem and see this thing that has happened, which the Lord has told us about."	Luke 2:29–30
Simeon	"We saw his star when it rose and have come to worship him."	Luke 2:15

Answer on page 16

The Nativity

The word *nativity* refers to the time of a person's birth. At Christmas, we use that word when we talk about Jesus' birthday. Many people set up a scene with special ornaments to represent the different people who were part of the Bible's story of Jesus' birth.

Use the number code to color this nativity scene.

Places in the Christmas Story

Do you remember what happened at these places in the Christmas story?

Circle the words hidden forwards, backwards, up, down, or diagonally.

M	B	C	Y	T	I	A	F	J	U	D	E	A	K	D	O	L	S	L	J	R
Y	O	A	S	P	F	I	G	I	S	Q	O	W	T	O	G	Z	I	Y	O	T
G	E	Q	X	W	N	M	F	J	O	A	T	B	L	K	A	S	M	M	Z	M
Y	A	O	X	E	Q	D	D	Z	T	Y	Y	E	I	V	T	M	A	B	O	E
Q	D	L	V	A	E	E	N	K	I	M	U	R	M	X	M	N	C	F	Z	R
X	Q	A	I	C	O	C	D	X	N	D	O	R	O	P	W	A	G	Y	H	J
Z	E	I	Q	L	G	R	K	A	E	G	V	X	X	O	L	W	U	M	E	E
H	P	Q	N	D	E	I	T	J	V	W	G	G	R	M	S	E	V	R	L	G
P	T	F	F	R	D	E	N	L	K	Y	Z	L	A	H	M	P	U	G	Y	Y
K	K	L	W	W	C	A	E	Z	S	I	D	H	Y	P	X	S	C	R	K	P
Z	H	W	H	R	N	B	B	Y	L	K	F	T	Q	N	A	K	R	O	F	T
H	V	Q	F	U	K	W	H	M	S	U	E	D	O	L	K	Y	N	B	U	I
J	M	O	Z	L	L	A	U	O	E	C	A	A	E	V	P	I	S	L	Q	D
W	S	P	U	K	P	K	Z	D	A	H	H	M	I	T	Y	X	E	I	C	R
Y	V	G	C	D	H	L	A	N	A	J	E	D	U	E	S	A	L	R	R	P
N	A	Z	A	R	E	T	H	L	P	E	O	L	L	A	R	A	M	K	F	W
V	V	P	Q	V	X	C	E	B	Y	C	K	P	H	S	F	R	E	L	S	N
X	D	D	Q	K	M	C	C	Y	C	Z	Y	D	I	T	N	M	K	E	R	E
R	K	X	L	M	A	N	Y	N	M	V	G	H	X	A	E	O	B	O	H	T
F	I	E	L	D	S	X	E	B	O	R	E	V	U	Y	Z	B	U	Q	S	T

BETHLEHEM
JUDEA
JERUSALEM
EGYPT
ISRAEL
NAZARETH
GALILEE
THE EAST
TEMPLE
ROMAN WORLD
FIELDS
HEAVEN

Answer on page 16

Jesus Is Born!

Jesus was born in a stable. Mary didn't have a crib, so she put her baby to sleep in a manger—a feeding bin for animals. God sent His only Son to the world in a simple way, so everyone could know how much He loves us.

Look closely at these two pictures of the nativity scene. Find 16 things that are different.

Answer on page 16

A Night to Remember

These ornaments tell the story of Jesus' birth, but someone made some mistakes!

Read each sentence. If the sentence is true, color the ornament. If the sentence is false, then cross out the wrong words and write the correct ones. Read Luke 2:1–20 to check your answers.

Answer on page 16

The Best Christmas Gift

Christmas is a wonderful celebration! In all the excitement, we want to remember the reason for our joy. That reason is found in the words the angel told the shepherds the night Jesus was born.

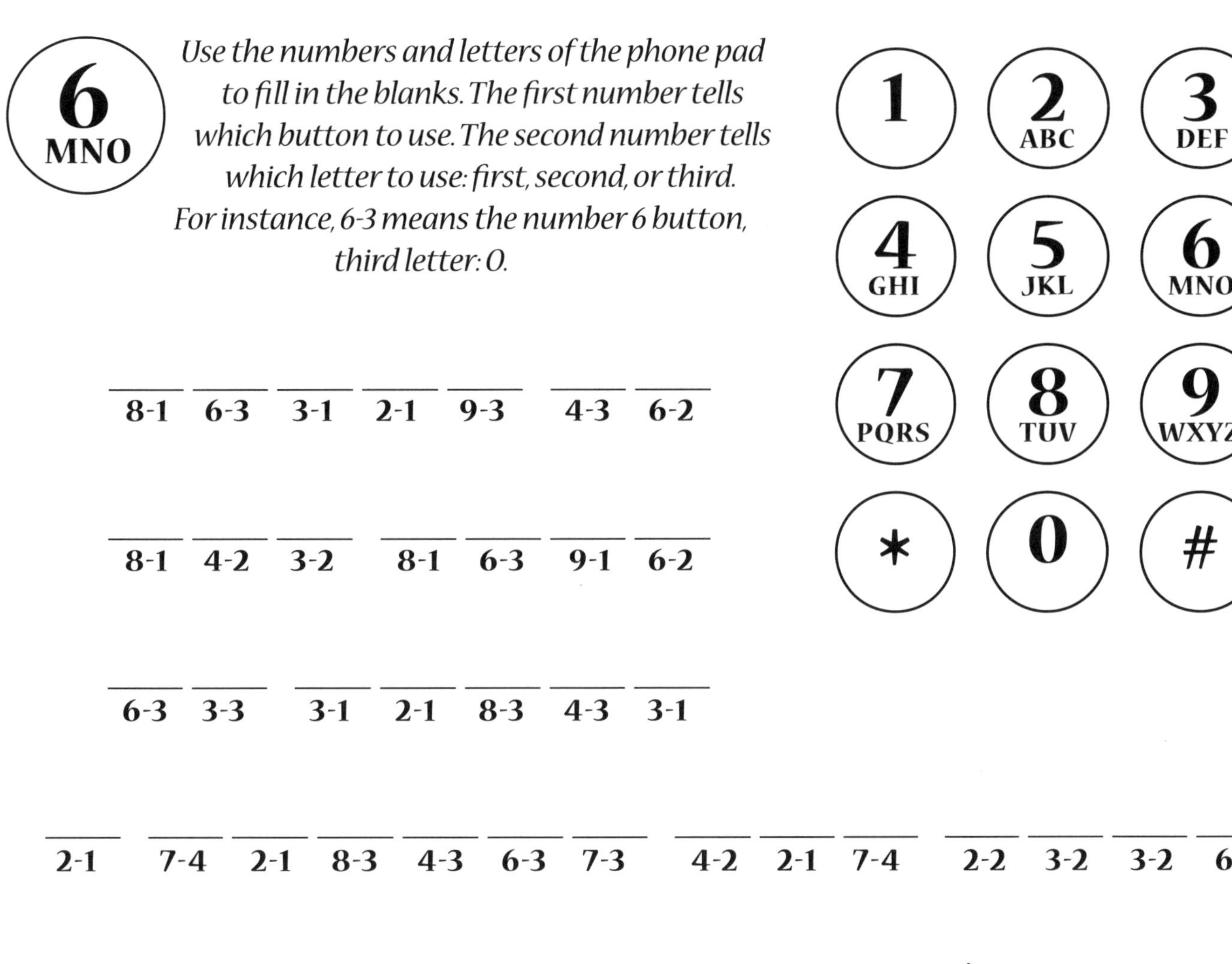

Use the numbers and letters of the phone pad to fill in the blanks. The first number tells which button to use. The second number tells which letter to use: first, second, or third. For instance, 6-3 means the number 6 button, third letter: O.

___ ___ ___ ___ ___   ___ ___
8-1 6-3 3-1 2-1 9-3   4-3 6-2

___ ___ ___   ___ ___ ___ ___
8-1 4-2 3-2   8-1 6-3 9-1 6-2

___ ___   ___ ___ ___ ___ ___
6-3 3-3   3-1 2-1 8-3 4-3 3-1

___   ___ ___ ___ ___ ___ ___   ___ ___ ___   ___ ___ ___ ___
2-1   7-4 2-1 8-3 4-3 6-3 7-3   4-2 2-1 7-4   2-2 3-2 3-2 6-2

___ ___ ___ ___   ___ ___   ___ ___ ___;   ___ ___
2-2 6-3 7-3 6-2   8-1 6-3   9-3 6-3 8-2   4-2 3-2

___ ___   ___ ___ ___   ___ ___ ___ ___ ___ ___ ___,
4-3 7-4   8-1 4-2 3-2   6-1 3-2 7-4 7-4 4-3 2-1 4-2

___ ___ ___   ___ ___ ___ ___. Luke 2:11 (NIV)
8-1 4-2 3-2   5-3 6-3 7-3 3-1

Answer on page 16

Answer Page

Page 2

Page 3

Across	Down
3. given	1. counselor
5. shoulders	2. everlasting
7. father	3. God
8. prince	4. government
9. angel	6. child
10. son	8. peace

Page 4

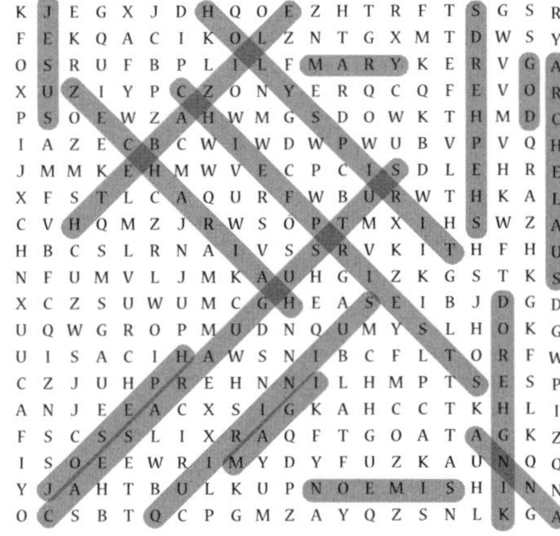

Page 5

1. An Angel Visits Mary
2. A Trip to Bethlehem
3. Jesus Is Born!
4. Angels Praise God
5. Shepherds Visit Jesus
6. Wise Men Bring Gifts

Page 6

1. Luke 1:11–13, 19–20; Gabriel; Zechariah; You will have a son.

2. Luke 1:26–38; Gabriel; Mary; You will give birth to God's Son Jesus.

3. Matthew 1:20–24: Angel of the Lord; Joseph; Don't be afraid to get married. Mary will give birth to God's Son Jesus.

4. Luke 2:8–12; Angel of the Lord; Shepherds; Jesus has been born!

5. Luke 2:13–14; Heavenly Host; Shepherds; Glory to God in the highest.

6. Matthew 2:13; Angel of the Lord; Joseph; Take Mary and Jesus to Egypt.

Page 7

Page 8

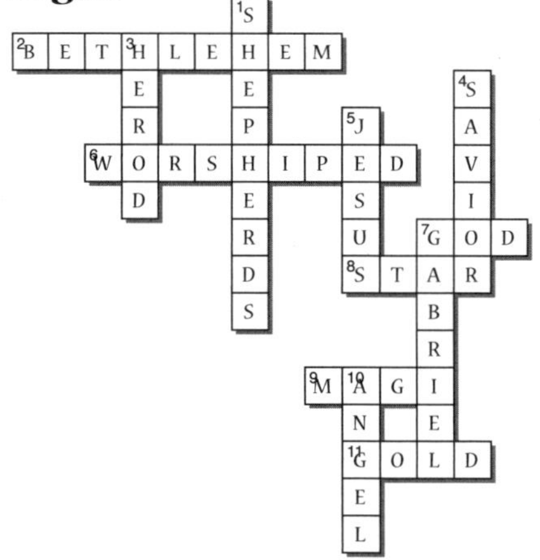

Page 9

You will conceive and give birth to a son, and you are to call him Jesus. He will be great and will be called the Son of the Most High. *Luke 1:31–32 (NIV)*

Page 10

Page 12

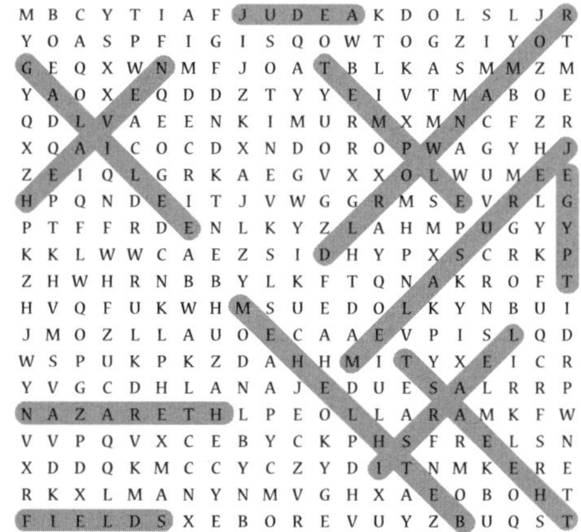

Page 13

Page 14

1. Moses' should be David's

3. straw should be cloths

4. far away should be nearby

6. "Bless the Lord" should be "Glory to God"

7. morning should be night

Page 15

Today in the town of David a Savior has been born to you; he is the Messiah, the Lord. *Luke 2:11 (NIV)*